HOW TO MARKET YOUR BOOK

LYNN MORRISON

Fairlight Books

First published by Fairlight Books 2020

Fairlight Books
Summertown Pavilion, 18–24 Middle Way, Oxford, OX2 7LG

A CIP catalogue record for this book is available from the British Library

ISBN 978-1-912054-44-2
www.fairlightbooks.com

Cover designed by Amanda Weiss

Printed and bound in Great Britain by TJ International Ltd, Padstow, Cornwall

CONTENTS

INTRODUCTION

The last decade has ushered in an incredible amount of change to the publishing industry. From traditional publishing houses to indie presses, from hybrid models to self-publishing, authors now have a number of routes to market to choose from. This broadening of the marketplace has led to millions of new books being released each year. It requires not only stellar writing but also a well-crafted marketing strategy and a lot of luck to ensure that a book has a chance of standing out among the masses. Contracting with a publishing house might provide access to marketing advice and support, but unless you are J. K. Rowling, the reality is that these days you are unlikely to get much beyond some initial launch support, even from mainstream publishers.

Every author I interviewed for this guide said that they had taken a very hands-on approach to promoting their book, and ultimately their hard work played a large role in driving book sales. It wasn't just self-published authors who worried about marketing strategies. Agents and publishers alike are asking authors what they will do to promote their book. 'Nothing' is no longer an acceptable answer.

As a debut or emerging author, getting access to credible and qualified marketing support is often well beyond budget constraints. By the time you've made it past the gauntlets of writing a first draft and editing it into something fit for public consumption, marketing the book is often the last thing on anyone's mind. Often authors are left to muddle through and hope for the best.

With over twenty years' experience and a Master's degree in marketing, there are very few marketing and promotional tactics I haven't seen or used over the years. The approach to developing a strategy, determining a budget and eventually identifying and executing tactics is exactly the same regardless of what product I am promoting. The tactics themselves will change, but the methodology for selecting them and tracking their effectiveness is the same.

It wasn't until I sat down for lunch with Louise Boland, CEO of Fairlight Books, an indie publishing house that specialises in debut and emerging literary fiction, that I realised how I could use my knowledge to help other authors. As we debated the merits of the different publishing options and chatted about marketing tactics over a plate of hummus, Louise commented that she wished her authors had access to all of the knowledge I had gained through experience and outreach. By the time the pitta bread ran out, the idea for this book had been born. We wanted to provide debut and emerging authors with a resource they could use to build up a plan for marketing their book, regardless of how they chose to publish it.

In putting together this guide, I've reached out to successful authors on both sides of the pond – some who have been traditionally published and others who have chosen to self-publish. I've included a wide variety of genres and provided examples from all available publishing channels. I've broken down the marketing process into individual tactics, providing both an overview of how you can execute these tactics as part of your book marketing strategy and real-life examples from authors who have used them with success.

If you are unsure about where to start when it comes to putting together a marketing plan, I recommend reading the book all the way through so that you can gain an understanding of what options are available and identify which ones may suit you best. If you are further along in your planning, you may find it more useful to skip around between chapters, learning more about the tactics that you hope to include. There is enough information on each option to enable you to determine which ones you can carry out on your own and which ones may require professional support or additional research.

If I could offer only one piece of personal advice, it would be to pick and choose the tactics that best align with your genre and with your own personality. Marketing and promotion take time and energy. You'll find the process a lot more fun if you spend it using tactics you enjoy and playing to your own personal strengths.

CHAPTER ONE

What Is Book Marketing?

Book marketing, in its most basic form, simply means getting the word out about your book. There are a number of marketing and promotional tactics you can use to accomplish this task. Before you rush off to tell the world about your book, you will want to take the time to put together a marketing plan.

A marketing plan outlines which tactics you intend to use, when you will use them and how much you will spend, in time and/or money, to do so. A marketing plan gives you an overall vision of how you will promote your book, and also breaks that vision down into bite-size pieces.

Why do you need a marketing plan? Simple: people won't buy your book unless they have heard about it. With such a large number of books out there, there is huge competition for readers' attention. Marketers often mention the 'rule of seven' – people need to see your book an average of seven different times before they will purchase it.

For this reason, getting your book into bookstores or online stores where people will see it is not enough. All authors, both traditionally published and self-published, have to earn the right to a prominent position in a bookstore or online store. You can earn this place either through strong publisher relationships, through winning prizes or through sales.

Often bookstores decide to stock a book and put it in a prominent position because they see people are talking about it, particularly if they see a lot of social media coverage of the book. You must make people want to buy it before they walk into a shop or browse an online store. You want to encourage bookstores to think it would be a great idea to stock your book and put it in a prominent position.

Therefore, a key cornerstone of your marketing plan is going to be finding ways to get people talking about the book. You should start with your circle of friends and acquaintances, no matter how small that circle might be. In today's connected world, it is becoming ever easier to see your circle of influence multiplied many times over. These days, social media is an essential part of this.

If you already have a social media following, you're off to a great start. But if social media scares you or you feel embarrassed by how few followers you have, don't worry – Chapter Seven has lots of details about how to get started.

At the end of the day, it doesn't matter how many followers you have. What matters is how much they engage with you on social platforms. Every time one of your followers shares or writes a post promoting your book within their circle of friends and acquaintances, your reach is exponentially increased. Think of social media as ripples from dropping a pebble into a pool.

As you put together your plan, you will ideally want to break it into three stages: pre-publication, launch and ongoing promotion. But it is never too late to start marketing, so don't give up if your book has already launched.

This guide will help you understand the most common book marketing tactics, ranging from social media to book tours, public speaking to professional reviews, newsletters and more. You can use these tactics to build up your plan, identifying the right time and budget to spend on them.

CHAPTER TWO

Understanding Your Marketplace

Understanding genre conventions and how different genres are marketed can be fundamental to the success of your book. By reading a large selection of titles, you can identify which authors write with a similar voice or produce stories that would appeal to your target audience. You can affirm your genre selection, or you may discover that your book would fit better under a different category. Researching the market for the genre your book best fits into is the first step in building up your marketing plan.

Step 1: Research which books are selling (and which are not)

Once you have determined which genre your book falls into, do extensive research both in brick-and-mortar bookstores and on online sites to identify which books in that category are selling well. Make a list of titles and authors that have achieved commercial and/or critical success.

Step 2: Investigate the competition

Now comes the heavy-lifting phase of your research: investigation. I recommend you create a spreadsheet to help you track your work and make it easier to identify patterns. Within your spreadsheet, start by listing all of the relevant authors in one column. The next column could include specific titles. From there, you should create a column for each marketing tactic you find these authors using. Do they have a website? Can you subscribe to a newsletter? How active is their social media? Make a note of which tactics they are employing, and to what degree.

Once you have compiled your spreadsheet, you could try to connect in some way with all of the authors you have identified. Follow them on social media, subscribe to their newsletters and check their schedules to see if they are attending any events in your area. Start saving examples of marketing activities that inspire you or attract your interest. At this point, you should be thinking about your circle of influencers. Authors can be extremely generous and helpful to other authors. Finding ways to connect with them in a genuine fashion can be valuable when you are looking for endorsers or established authors who might co-host events.

Step 3: Building your plan and setting your budget

Now that you have a firm understanding of what marketing tactics authors in your genre are using, you are ready to start building up your marketing plan. Unless you have an endless amount of time or money, you will want to divide your plan into three categories: Must Do, Should Do and Could Do.

Your Must Do items are the ones that all or nearly all of the authors you identified are using. Nowadays nearly everyone has at least a basic website and some sort of social media presence. You will want to make sure that you have the same foundation to help establish your credentials.

Your Should Do tactics are those that many of your fellow authors are using to connect with readers and promote their books. For example, you may identify that a specific social media platform is popular with your audience. Likewise, you might find that in-person events are more important. These will become the next layer of your plan and help guide your budget choices.

The final category, Could Do, is your wish list. This is where you will list some of the more interesting or unusual marketing tactics you've seen your fellow authors use with success. The items in this category don't necessarily have to be expensive to produce – they are simply nice-to-haves that you can consider if budget and time allow.

Now that you have created your categories and divided up your tactics, you should begin to cost them out. Budgets can be set from the bottom up, starting with a list of all of your desired activities and seeing how they total up.

Alternatively, you can work from the top down, deciding in advance how much you can afford to invest and then selecting the best way to allocate those funds. You don't need to have a final number in mind when you start if you are unsure.

Step 4: Balancing your budget against your sales forecast

This final step is the most important one when it comes to creating a marketing plan. A good marketing plan should never require more investment than it will generate in new sales and revenue. You should have a clear idea in mind of how much money you will make from the sales of your book, or of future books if you are planning to publish more than one.

This will be harder for traditionally published authors, as you probably will not have real-time access to your sales data. If your publishing company has a marketing team, you could ask to have a call or meeting with them to go through their marketing and promotion plans. You can work with them to discuss how your ideas could help and whether they are likely to generate new sales. Even if you don't have easy access to your sales data, it is still worthwhile tracking the costs of any marketing activity you would like to carry out and understanding the likely payback of your investment of time or money.

In interviewing authors for this book, the main horror stories I heard came from the ones who overinvested in their marketing tactics. Authors who spent thousands paying for high-profile publicity campaigns or who overspent on book tours expressed the most regret. It is better to start small or stay local, maximising your budget and your reach, than it is to splash out on an expensive national campaign that might fail to deliver.

Among all the authors I polled, both traditionally published and self-published, I found that on average they chose to spend around $2,500/£2,000 promoting their book, not including the value of their time. Most of the self-published authors had a specific break-even target in mind when deciding where to invest. If they felt that the target was unachievable, they put their money elsewhere.

When it comes to marketing planning and budgeting, you should set your personal sentiments aside and view the process with a critical business lens. Put together a mini business plan and imagine you are pitching it to an investor. If an outsider would poke holes in it or would decline to invest, then you shouldn't either.

CHAPTER THREE

Growing a Support Network

If writing a book is a solitary task, publishing and marketing one is not. To be successful in getting your book into the hands of a wider audience, you need a network of people who are willing to support you. Often, the best support you can get is from other writers. After all, who understands the ups and downs of writing, publishing and marketing a book better than someone else who has done it?

Regardless of where you are in your writing career, you should be focused on growing your network. Thankfully, this is much easier nowadays than it was in the past, with a large number of online groups popping up to support in-person events. There is ample opportunity to meet writers within your genre so that you can learn from their experiences, get advice and find chances to help one another out. You should always keep in mind that networking is a two-way street. For every bit of help you get, you should be ready to turn around and repay or pay forward the favour.

Below are some suggestions of places where you can network with other writers and industry professionals.

Local writing groups

Sometimes the safest and best place to start looking for a group is in your own backyard. Local writing groups can provide a safe space for you to share your work and make connections with potential writing partners and mentors. Local groups have the benefit of being convenient in terms of location while still providing a face-to-face encounter.

When looking for a local group, be upfront about what you are hoping to get out of it. It is important to find a group with similar expectations and where everyone is willing to read your genre.

Online groups

Social media has opened up new avenues for connection, and writing groups are no exception. There are hundreds – possibly thousands – of writing and reading groups online where writers can network with others within their genre. While many of these groups are public and can be found by using the platform's search function, others are fiercely guarded private enclaves. The best way to gain access to those is by asking other writers.

If you are completely new to online writing groups and don't personally know any writers, the best place to start might be connecting with an author you admire. Many authors now host their own social media groups where they interact with readers and fans. You can start by joining an author's fan group and getting to know the author in a friendly, supportive manner. Once you've had a chance to get to know them, and they you, it would acceptable to message the author, let them know you are writing within their genre and ask them if they can recommend any good online networking groups. There is no obligation for them to reply, but you may find them willing to point you in the right direction.

You can also use popular writing hashtags like #writers, #amwriting or #writingcommunity in searches to find other writers who are active online. Using these kinds of hashtags when posting content on social media is an excellent way to reach people who aren't following you and vice versa. Commenting, sharing or retweeting content you like is an easy way to begin connecting with other writers.

Industry organisations

If you are searching for something more formal, you may want to look into industry organisations. You can find everything from genre-specific groups to author community groups, all the way up to wider writing community groups. Some of these groups have a membership threshold, such as a minimum number of books published or annual sales, and most of them require annual dues. In exchange, you can access not only their member network but also courses, informational guides, agent and publisher introductions and even legal support.

As a debut or emerging author, you may also want to look into any programmes these groups may offer specifically for you. Some groups sponsor first book awards or have special membership types that allow you to join before your book is published.

Festivals and conferences

Festivals, conferences and other annual events should be on your consideration list. In both the UK and the US, there are a large number of well-respected events taking place, including those focused on the craft of writing, and genre-specific or regional options.

Festivals and conferences offer unique opportunities to network with well-respected authors, agents and publishers, in addition to their author interviews, panels and educational sessions. You may get the chance to meet your dream author or agent in person and to ask some of those questions you've always wanted to ask.

Many festivals and conferences also include competitions, which can be particularly interesting for debut and emerging authors. Even if you don't win the grand prize, you may still get valuable critiques or attract the attention of new readers. Winning a prize can open many doors, as covered in Chapter Thirteen.

How Adam Hamdy uses festivals to market his books

British author and screenwriter Adam Hamdy is best known as the author of the *Pendulum* trilogy, an epic series of conspiracy thriller novels. His work has gained the attention of writing legends such as James Patterson, as well as television and movie producers. He is also the co-founder of Capital Crime, a London-based annual crime and thriller festival. I interviewed Adam to learn more about his experience with networking, why he launched a festival and what advice he has for debut authors.

Adam began by explaining his interest in festivals. 'I went to my first literary festival in 2016, just before my debut novel, *Pendulum*, was published. My publisher sent me to the Theakston Old Peculier Crime Writing Festival to promote the book and build relationships within the author and publishing community.'

When asked why he decided to launch a new festival, he said, 'David Headley and I started Capital Crime because we thought London needed a big crime and thriller festival. London has the biggest concentration of readers anywhere in the country, but they don't seem well served by literary festivals.'

He had no hesitation in encouraging writers, or even those still aspiring to write, to put festivals at the top of their networking list. 'I would advise aspiring authors to go to festivals as soon as they're able. Most festivals feature discussion about the craft and business of writing, so authors can learn a lot. I wish I'd gone to festivals when I first started writing because I think I could have saved myself a lot of heartache.

'Literary festivals are generally very inclusive and accessible and it's easy to approach authors and ask for advice. I can't imagine going to a film festival and bumping into Steven Spielberg, but you can bump into Ian Rankin or Martina Cole in the bar. It's one of the few creative industries where top-tier talent makes itself accessible to the general public, so definitely go as an attendee.'

He had a great tip for meeting people, saying, 'The best way to get your foot in the door is to hang around the bar. Every author was once an aspiring author and most will be happy to give hints and advice, providing you don't take liberties with their time or generosity.'

Festivals and conferences sometimes include promotional opportunities. I asked Adam when the best time is for a new author to investigate these. He replied, 'The correct time for an author to introduce him- or herself to a festival organiser is when he or she has a debut novel heading towards publication. If it's going to be traditionally published, the author's publisher will usually make the festival organiser aware of the debut, but it doesn't hurt to connect directly as well.'

Adam's festival Capital Crime runs an annual competition for unpublished works. Adam listed the benefits to participants, beyond the prize itself: 'All the authors who were shortlisted for the Capital Crime DHH New Voices Award saw increased interest in their work from agents and publishers. In a world of authors clamouring to be noticed, being shortlisted for a prize can provide a real boost.'

Adam outlined a helpful list of dos and don'ts that any new or aspiring writer should take to heart:

- Do network with authors. We're a friendly bunch and generally happy to provide advice.
- Do read a lot. It will help inform your writing and keep you abreast of trends within the marketplace.
- Don't be rude. I'm amazed at the number of aspiring authors who take rejection personally and lash out. You never know when a relationship might become important, and just because an agent rejects this book doesn't mean he or she wouldn't be interested in another one.

- Don't try to become an author unless it's in your blood. It's a demanding and often painful existence, so you need to really love the process of writing to make the downsides worth living with.

Finally, I asked Adam to provide his one piece of advice to debut and emerging authors. He said, 'Don't rush. Take time to find out who you are as a storyteller. The shelves are full of romance novels. What makes yours different? What does your story bring to the world that makes it unique and why are you the person to tell it? Once you've answered those questions, spend time finding your voice. Every storyteller has a style. What's yours? Why is it unique? Then, if you can, invest in honing your craft. There are a lot of good writing courses out there. I teach at Arvon, which runs an impressive range of residential courses. It also offers grants for people who need them. Invest the time and energy in making your writing the best it can be.'

CHAPTER FOUR

Preparation for Publication

When it comes to preparing for launch day, the longer timescales associated with publishing work in your favour. Much of the heavy lifting of a book marketing campaign is done before the publication date.

Step 1: Preparation – three to six months before launch

Your marketing efforts should begin three to six months before your expected publication date. If you are close to or beyond your publication date, don't despair. Take a look at the pre-publication activities to determine which of them you can do quickly but still effectively, and add these to your post-publication plan.

Before you begin spreading the word about your forthcoming work, you want to make sure that anyone searching for information about you can easily connect with you. The best place to start is with an author website. You will need to buy a domain name and select a website host. Once you have done so, you can choose to build your website yourself on a DIY platform like WordPress, SquareSpace or Wix, or you can hire a website developer to do it for you. Don't feel that you must spend a fortune to do it right; the DIY platforms are user-friendly and many offer author-specific website templates that are ready to use. Your website should at a minimum include information on your book, links to buy it, your bio and media contact information.

With your website in place, you should next consider social media. If you are social media-shy, don't worry. You don't have to use all the platforms. I've included a short guide to social media at the end of this chapter if you need more information on how authors typically use it. Select the platforms where you will feel most comfortable and which best align with your audience and marketing plans. Social media, if used right, will not only help you build relationships with readers, but will also amplify your marketing when readers, family and friends share your posts with their followers.

Next you should consider starting a newsletter. A newsletter subscriber list can be the most important marketing asset you own. I've covered newsletters in depth in Chapter Nine.

The final part of your preparation is to start identifying your key supporters or influencers. If you are able to, you should use this time to contact people who you think might be prepared convince them to take the leap and make a purchase. [Yo]u can find more information on reviews in Chapter Six.

If you have a publisher, make sure you check you are not [du]plicating effort or doubling up on any communications to [r]eviewers.

Now is the time to follow up with your endorsers for quotes to be used on your book cover or in the blurb, and to pass them on to your publisher or your cover designer. The sooner you can get these reviews to them, the more likely it is that they will be able to include them on the cover, inside the book or in the promotional material sent to bookstores.

Step 4: Generating excitement – two weeks before launch

With less than a month to go, now is the time to bring the excitement to a crescendo. You should plan daily promotional activities for your social media accounts and consider sending a weekly email to your newsletter subscribers. Use a variety of messages to keep these activities from growing stale. For example, you might share a review one day, announce a new endorsement the next and share a short excerpt on the third day. Make sure you keep the messaging fresh and interesting so that you don't alienate your followers.

to read an early copy of your book and provide a positive 'endorsement' (those little words of praise you see on book covers). Endorsements are lovely if they come from your mother, but better if they come from someone influential. For example, you might consider contacting a well-known personality, a popular author within your genre, a person with an academic record in the subject or someone who has a large social media following. If you have any connections within the press, you may wish to reach out to them to request a review of your book. Be aware that the number of pages in newspapers and magazines devoted to book reviews is falling, while the number of books being published is rising. There's stiff competition for these reviews, so it's best to manage your expectations.

If you are traditionally published, you should be able to ask your publisher to send a limited number of your reviewers a bound proof copy (a version printed before the proofreading stage) or a PDF file of the book. If you are self-publishing, you will need to arrange to have some early release versions for this purpose.

Step 2: Getting people talking about your book – three months before launch

At the three-month-out mark, you will want to announce your book to family, friends and followers. Authors frequently choose to do this with a 'cover reveal', showing the cover on social media or in a newsletter for the first time, or by sharing a blurb (a punchy and enticing short description of the book). Think of this announcement like a movie trailer: you want to drum up excitement, give people some idea of what the book is about and let them know when they can expect to find it for sale. If your book is traditionally published, you should coordinate all of these activities with your publisher. They may provide further support on their own website and social channels or by releasing information to industry press.

At three months out, your support network starts to come into its own. Many authors refer to this as their 'street team': a group of people who you can depend on to help you with promoting your book, either online or in person. They may have engaging social media channels where they can share information on your book. They might run a book club or have relationships with local bookstores where they can convince people to buy your book in bulk. Your street team will help you quickly generate reviews for your book, either on sales platforms such as Amazon or on book review websites such as Goodreads.

Step 3: Gathering reviews – two months before launch

At least two months before your book is released, you will want to focus your attention on getting reader reviews. You can facilitate this by distributing Advance Reader Copies (ARCs).

When it comes to handing out ARC need to be realistic about the outcome. receives one will read it. Fewer still will review. Finally, but critically, not all of the positive. You want to make sure that your re enough time to fit reading the book into their sc that they will be available and able to post a revie launch date.

Your aim here is to get as many reviews as possib the online world around the time of your book's public date. No one can post a review on Amazon before the bc is available for purchase. However, this is not the case fc Goodreads, where reviews can be posted in advance of publication. Your ARC readers can help you get reviews onto your book's page on these sites as quickly as possible, whether in the weeks leading up to your publication date or, in the case of Amazon, on launch date and within the first week.

You may also choose to send your book to professional review websites. In this case, you should check out their guidelines and follow their timelines and submission processes.

Early reviews are a critical part of your eventual success or failure, particularly as a debut or emerging author. As most readers will be unfamiliar with your work, seeing other readers validate that a book is well written and engaging can

Step 5: Launch week

Although the actual launch day will be the date circled in your calendar, your marketing plan needs to stretch the launch activities into at least a week. Your first week of book marketing will be split into two areas of focus: gathering reviews and support behind the scenes, and carrying out promotional activities.

Now that your book has been born into the world, you should be checking in with the members of your street and review teams. Have they completed the promotional activities they committed to? Have they posted reviews to Amazon, Goodreads and any other platform they use? Checklists are your best friends – prep lists of team members and their commitments in advance. This will make it much easier for you to keep track of who has delivered and who has not. Expect to have some plans fall through, but make a note not to include those individuals in future plans.

Wondering which social media platform is right for you? Here are some examples of how writers use them, beyond basic promotion:

Twitter

Thanks to hashtags and public profiles, Twitter is a great networking tool for writers. You can use hashtags to discover new authors and identify potential agents and publishers. You can jump into conversations, discover what is attracting interest and keep up with the latest releases from your favourite writers and publishers. Twitter is also useful for connecting with bookstores, giving you a chance to see what they are promoting to their customers.

Instagram

Instagram's visual format gives gorgeous book covers a place to shine. There is a whole world of 'bookstagrammers' living on the platform, using photography to share their favourite books with their audience of followers.

Facebook

If you are looking for a place to find private writers' groups and to promote events, Facebook is your top choice. There are public, private and secret groups of writers meeting on Facebook every day to share advice, commiserate over challenges and celebrate successes. Facebook's events tool is particularly useful when promoting in-person or online events to a wide audience. It allows event organisers to leverage attendees' social connections to attract more people.

LinkedIn

LinkedIn's professional networking environment is useful to writers looking for expert sources. You can use its search functions to find professionals with the expertise you need to write your book. These might include potential interview sources, cover designers, editors and more.

YouTube

Any author interested in adding public speaking to their promotional pack should start with YouTube. You can upload highlight reels to share with event organisers, or even post videos of your presentations. YouTube is also home to 'booktubers', who share and discuss their favourite reads in videos posted to their channels.

CHAPTER FIVE

Book Tours

Every marketer is trained in the 4 Ps: Product, Price, Place and Promotion. With your book at the printer and your price already set, Place is the next item on your planning list. That place is most likely a bookstore. For this reason, bookstore tours are often the first item on an author's marketing plan. You expect to turn up and find that the store has filled the room with people who are eager to hear and buy your words.

Unfortunately, the reality of a bookstore tour couldn't be more different. Bookstores can provide you with a place, but they won't provide you with a ready-made crowd of listeners. Like most book marketing tactics, unless you are already a well-known household name or have written a book that a major publishing house is throwing its weight behind, that responsibility falls on the shoulders of the author. And that's assuming they're willing to let you in the door in the first place.

I've given dozens of store-based presentations in my career, learning along the way what steps are needed to make them into a success.

Step 1: Make your book available to bookstores

This step seems obvious, but it is particularly critical for self-published authors and can sometimes be problematic for authors whose books are published by a very small indie publisher. If your printed book is produced by an online book retailer, your local brick-and-mortar bookstore may not easily be able or willing to order printed copies of your book. You must either make your book available for order by a book distributor or wholesaler which the shop has an account with or convince them to accept books directly from you. This is also true of any bookstores you might visit to ask if they will stock your book. Be as polite as you can and remember that many bookstores are small businesses working to survive in a tough marketplace. They are under no obligation to stock your book if they don't think it will sell in their store.

Step 2: Prepare a pitch

Before you contact any stores, you need to prepare a one-page overview of you and your book. In the industry this is called an AI sheet (or Advanced Information sheet). If you have a publisher, they should be able to send you a copy of the AI sheet their sales reps are using when they visit stores. If you are self-published, you will need to create this for yourself.

The AI should be one page only and should include a high-quality image of your cover, your blurb, details on how the store can buy the book, a short author bio and any impressive endorsements you have gathered or prizes your book has won or been nominated for. If you cannot afford a designer, you can use free tools like Canva to ensure that your AI looks professional.

Step 3: Contact your local bookstore first

It's always best to start with a friendly audience. Go into the store in person and ask to speak with whoever arranges their events. Introduce yourself as a local author who regularly visits their store, provide them with a printed copy of your pitch pack and ask if they would be willing to consider hosting your local launch event. You may also want to add an estimate of the number of people you can get to attend. This will help them judge whether the event is worth the effort on their part.

Step 4: Contact other bookstores

Book tours are challenging for new authors who don't have an existing readership base or a large, loyal following. You may be better off holding one well-organised book launch than spreading your efforts across a larger tour. If you think about expanding beyond your local area, focus on locations where you have a local connection who can help you promote the event. This might be a friend or relative, a member of your street team or a loyal reader. Contact that person and get suggestions of bookstores local to them. With their permission, you can include their information when you begin contacting the stores.

If you don't have a local contact, you may want to look at local authors who write in your genre. Could you contact them about co-hosting an event? Could they provide an introduction for you or serve as the moderator for a Q&A?

Before contacting the store, check their website to see if they offer any guidance on preferred pitch methods. This can help you avoid a quick 'no' simply because you have used the wrong format for your request. If they have a preferred approach, use it.

Step 5: Promoting your event

The burden is on you to fill the seats in the room. Start by asking the bookstore what they typically do for promotion. This will allow you to avoid duplicating effort. You could ask them if they will list the event on their website, share it on social media, create social media event invitations and issue notes to local press and event listings. Whatever they are not doing, you need to do.

Use your own network and social media accounts to promote the event. You can share the bookstore's promotion or you can create your own. If you are a doing a series of events, it will likely make sense for you to have your own event listings.

You can build up a template schedule for promoting your event. For example, you could announce the event as soon as it is booked, then schedule reminder messages for thirty, fifteen and ten days before the event. You will want to promote the event more heavily in the few days leading up to it so that people don't forget to attend.

Step 6: After the event

After the event is over, send a personalised thank you card to the store rep who organised the event. This will help build a foundation for returning in the future. You can use your newsletter and social channels to thank everyone who came out for the event.

Make sure you follow up on any commitments you made to readers at the event, and if you collected email addresses, add them to your mailing list.

Extra tip: promote your book's availability in brick-and-mortar bookstores

Bookstores promote authors who promote them. If you have a website, make sure you include links to all available booksellers, including websites that list independent shops. You are more likely to get a yes from an indie shop if they see that you support their place in the industry.

How Elly Lonon used book tours to promote her book

Successful freelance writer Elly Lonon hit gold when she launched her 'Amongst the Liberal Elite' column on famed satire site McSweeney's Internet Tendencies. Having built an audience of fans, she decided to turn the column into an illustrated book that would follow her fictional liberal elite couple on a journey around the US. The end result was the graphic novel *Amongst the Liberal Elite: The Road Trip Exploring Societal Inequities Solidified by Trump (RESIST).*

Elly's outgoing personality and highly topical subject matter perfectly aligned to help her build a successful bookstore tour. I reached out to her to understand how she secured those coveted event slots.

Elly started by explaining her choice of publisher: 'I signed with a small indie press who distribute through Penguin Random House. This gave me access to major booksellers, but also meant that I didn't have a large marketing team I could lean upon. I had to do most of the bookstore tour heavy lifting.'

Before contacting stores, she made sure her website included all booksellers and a link to IndieBound (not just

Amazon) to show her support of independent stores. She leveraged her connection to a traditional publishing house and reached out to other writers she respected to secure blurbs for the book jacket. She later gained a review from the *New York Times*, which she uses in her promotional efforts.

'I came up with the idea of promoting the events as "In Conversation With…", always partnering with someone from the area. I reached out to bloggers, social activists and other authors in my genre. As my book is political satire, I tied my tour in with the US midterm elections. I'd help promote local candidates and "get out the vote" activities, or would debate political issues. This gave me several angles to use in promotion.'

Elly used the events as opportunities to reach out to other authors and introduce herself. 'I found people to be very supportive and friendly. Even those who said no to co-hosting an event were happy to share suggestions or meet for a chat. When an author said yes, the bookstores were pleased to have two or more books they could promote at the event – effectively twice the opportunity for sales. It turned out to be a really good way to grow my literary circle.'

I asked Elly if she had any parting advice for fellow authors. She said, 'I think my biggest mistake was that I waited too long for other people to step in and market my book for me. I missed out on early press opportunities through thinking someone else would do my PR.'

CHAPTER SIX

Interviews and Speaking Opportunities

If you are looking for new opportunities to promote your book in person, you might want to take a look at the business world. After all, finding promotional speaking slots for business leaders is much the same as booking in an author. In both cases, you have a product you want to promote and the event organisers have a calendar slot they need to fill.

Over the years, I've booked CEOs and Directors into any number of speaking engagements, from breakfast talks to brown-bag lunches, all the way up to centre stage. These incredibly busy executives with hourly rates well above my own always find time in their diaries to attend. Why? Because they know that speaking engagements drive sales, even if you never mention your product. The same holds true for book promo.

Before you set foot on stage, here are the things you need to do to make the most of any speaking opportunities:

Step 1: Finding your audience

Every good speech starts with the audience: who are they, where are they and what would they be interested in hearing? Think about your readers. Are you hitting a certain demographic? Do they all share a common interest or hobby? Grab a piece of paper and jot down as many characteristics as you can about your readers. Once you have this list, use it as a guide to where you might find them. For example, if you have written a middle-grade book, there's no point in booking yourself in at a pregnancy conference. You'd be better off at a middle school librarian's event.

If you aren't sure where to start, try looking up other authors in your genre. Are any of them on the speakers' circuit? If so, what types of events are they attending? This approach was particularly helpful to me when trying to book events for business leaders. I'd google the competitor's leader and look for events where they were being advertised. Don't be afraid to pitch events they've attended – most conference and event organisers want new speakers at each event.

Step 2: Preparing your speech

If this is your first time speaking in public in many years, I recommend that you write at least an outline of your speech before you begin your outreach. Nearly every event I've attended had a golden rule: ninety-five per cent of the content had to be informative and engaging, and no more than five per cent could be promotional. Think less about the content of your book and more about how you could identify a universal element within it to form the basis for a presentation.

For example, if your hero is a rule-breaker, you might create a talk that teaches the listener to think outside the box and to have the courage to defy societal constraints. Your presentation could also be about yourself. Have you over-come challenges or faced down fear in writing your book? Could you turn your story into an inspirational advice talk?

Keep working on your outline or draft until you have a clear picture of the audience's key takeaway. Will they laugh, cry, learn or perhaps even all three? This will form part of your pitch.

Step 3: Pitching event organisers

Now that you have a clear picture of your audience in mind, as well as some starting points for events, associations or conferences you could target and a speech outline, you are ready to start pitching. You have two options for your outreach: first, you can do it yourself; second, you can hire a PR agency or publicist. I have used both options in my career and suggest that you base your decision on your budget and on your personal comfort level.

I asked Holly Pither, founder of Tribe PR, a UK-based indie PR agency, how she would structure a speaker pitch. Holly regularly pitches her clients for speaker opportunities. The key, she says, is giving the team organising the speaker slot as much reassurance as possible. She explained, 'If you put on an event, be that a speaker slot, panel or Q&A with an author, you want to be assured that the person speaking will keep the audience entertained and won't fudge their words. When pitching out a speaker, I always make sure I send a sample online video to showcase that speaker or send them a snippet of recording of my client talking at a similar event. That way the event organisers can be sure that the speaker will do their event justice and will likely be keen to book them in ASAP rather than considering their options. In a world full of competing voices, all shouting very loudly, it's essential to make sure you cut through and a showcase speaker video can do just that.'

Step 4: Preparing for the big day
As your event date draws near, you'll undoubtedly be thinking about your speech. Make sure you practise it in front of an audience. It will help you refine your cadence and understand which parts are working well and which ones are not.

What you may not have in mind is your prep work for book sales. After all, the point of doing the speaking event is to move books. Ask your organiser to provide a small table for your use. You will want to arrange to have a stock of books on hand and the ability to take multiple forms of payment. If you can't or don't want to manage stock and sales, you can partner with a local bookstore. I would also recommend that you invest in a tablecloth and a pull-up banner you can carry around with you. They are relatively inexpensive (less than $125/£100) and are excellent advertising materials.

Step 5: At the event

When you arrive at the event, take a deep breath, hold it in and then let it out. Ninety-five per cent of the hard work is behind you. Locate your speaking area and your table and begin setting up your book display. Once your display table is arranged, walk around and introduce yourself to other attendees. Don't be afraid to tell them you've written a book.

Take a glass of water up with you when you go to speak and don't stress out if you forget a line of your speech. It's fine to pause for a moment and regroup, or even to make a joke out of it. At the end of your talk, let people know you'll be sticking around for a while and are happy to chat. Tell or show them where your table is located and invite them over for autographed copies of your book.

When the last person leaves, thank the organiser for the opportunity and ask them if they have any feedback to share.

Then put the whole event behind you and get to work on the next one.

How Andra Watkins uses public speaking to market her books

Ever since Andra was little, she always knew she wanted to be a performer. She loved being the centre of attention and watching the emotional reactions of her audience.

This desire to entertain led Andra to write her first book, *To Live Forever: An Afterlife Journey of Meriwether Lewis*. Since the book was set along the Natchez Trace, Andra came up with a unique promotional idea. She decided to take up the challenge of walking the entire highway, 444 gruelling miles, to hopefully capture local, regional and national press attention and promote her book. With her father on hand to ferry her back and forth to hotel rooms each day, she discovered much more than a promotional opportunity. She found herself facing universal challenges related to ageing parents and faltering relationships. When she got back home and her feet stopped swelling, she turned her adventure into a memoir. That book, *Not Without My Father: One Woman's 444-Mile Walk of the Natchez Trace*, made the *New York Times* Bestseller List.

Andra now has three novels, one memoir and one photography book published – plenty of content to promote while speaking at events. Her website showcases events stretching for months ahead. I reached out to her to find out what advice she'd give to debut and emerging authors who wish to follow in her footsteps.

Andra explained, 'I started by approaching groups who needed speakers to fill their thirty-minute slots on the regular. I didn't get paid for these, but I did find a captive audience.'

Civic clubs, Chambers of Commerce and local libraries are good examples of the types of organisations Andra targets.

I asked Andra how she puts her presentations together and whether she varies them for each group. She said, 'I build my talk in a modular storyteller style, designed to generate an emotional reaction. I can add or remove elements depending on the group and how much time I have. When I'm creating material, I always practise in front of a group, even if only family or friends. This helps me to see whether a bit is working or not. Don't be afraid to fall on your face in front of a friendly crowd to get it right.

'Outside of library groups, most attendees don't want to know about the process of writing. They want to see that you can tell a story. You are selling your ability. You need to practise and plan, take it very seriously. People often come up to me afterwards and say, "I want to buy your book because I loved your talk. If the book is half as good, I know that I'll enjoy it." My presentations are a performance, and require that level of energy.'

When asked for one piece of marketing advice for new authors, she said, 'You need to understand that everything is on you. If you aren't doing something to promote your book, no one else is either. Don't expect someone to do your marketing for you.'

CHAPTER SEVEN

Spreading the Word: Reviews, Blogs and Podcasts

When it comes to selling a product, there is one information source which consistently outranks all others: word of mouth. Individuals turn to friends, family, colleagues, social media connections and favourite influencers long before they do any other research. This is great news for authors who want to reach audiences without spending a small fortune.

Step 1: Identify your promoters

Well before your book arrives on the shelf, you need to start thinking about how you can garner reviews and recommendations. The process begins with identifying the right people to approach about promoting your book. You should divide these individuals into two categories: personal acquaintances and professional reviewers.

When it comes to friends and family, make sure you cast your net wider than your parents and cousins. Make a list of everyone who has ever expressed an interest in your writing and then narrow it down to those who have the largest number of social connections. These can be real-world connections, like membership of clubs or associations, or virtual connections through social media. This list is your primary target for personal recommendations.

With that done, you can turn your attention to professional reviewers. These could be people you find via platforms such as NetGalley, book review blogs and podcasts, and social media influencers in the 'bookstagrammer' category. Identify ten to twenty individuals you can reach out to. These should be influencers who regularly read your genre and are known for giving honest reviews. Whilst having a large number of followers can make one more appealing than another, don't fall prey to believing that all of their followers will see information about your book. As far as possible, check out how much engagement their content gets, and pick the ones who have a clear conversational connection with their audience.

Once you've made your selection, gather information on submission guidelines. Many professional reviewers do not accept unsolicited books. They may ask you to send in a pitch for consideration and only to send over copies of your book if requested. If you mail an unsolicited copy, it is more likely your book will go straight from the mailbox into the bin.

Step 2: Prepare your promotional materials

First and foremost, you will need advance copies of your book, in both electronic and print format. For printed copies, either ask your publisher for proof copies or, if self-publishing, order a larger batch when you run your print proofs. Assuming the cover is correctly printed, you can pass these copies along for people to take their own photographs. If you expect people to read the physical copies in order to prepare their review, make sure you have the materials well in advance.

With your Advance Reader Copies (ARCs) ready for distribution, you can now prepare your support materials to showcase your book cover, blurbs and endorsements. You will need an AI (Advanced Information) sheet you can easily distribute – this can be the same one-pager you use for bookstore outreach – and social media-friendly photos and images. You may also want to consider including a headshot if you have one.

Step 3: Coordinating a plan

Your word-of-mouth plan should be split across three stages: launch day, the first two weeks and everything else.

Although you may want to promote pre-sales, your actual publication date should mark the start of the bulk of your outreach activities. On day one, ask everyone on your friends, family and acquaintances list to post, send and share the news that your book is now available to the world. Think of it as a party invite: send a 'save the date' for their calendars, a full invite with all of the information they need to help you sell your book, and finally reminders in the days leading up to the big event. Publishing a book into the world is certainly cause for celebration – don't hesitate to treat it as such.

As you move into the category of professional reviewers, you can extend your timeline into the first two weeks. One popular idea is to host a blog or Instagram tour, appearing on a different site or account each day. You can publicise the schedule in advance and have fresh content to share on your own social channels every day. You should be prepared to support this with interviews or guest posts as needed.

Once your launch is behind you, turn your attention to an ongoing promotional strategy. You can reach out to new groups of professional reviewers, working to their schedules. Make notes on how followers react to your early promotion and add this information to your outreach messages. The more evidence you can provide to illustrate that your book is resonating with readers of your genre, the higher the likelihood that a professional reviewer will want to discuss it.

How The Paper Charm helps writers organise and run online book tours

The Paper Charm is a UK-based book marketing and content creation agency, helping writers find their voice in the book world. Its co-founders bonded over a love of books and realised that their backgrounds in marketing and IT provided the perfect combination for helping writers and publishers promote their books on- and offline. Together, they offer everything from influencer campaigns to social media coaching, book launches, and blog and bookstagram tours.

I reached out to The Paper Charm to learn what authors need to do to prep for an Instagram and blog tour.

The Paper Charm explained that the preparation work is pretty simple. 'The authors we work with don't really take part in or create content for the tours. We don't expect them to take photos or write posts. Author Q&As can be arranged but we feel the organic posts are always better. So it's important for the author to state what he/she expects as the result of the tour. Who do they want to target? What sort of influencers need to read/review/showcase their book? This is the sort of information the authors need to determine before booking a social media tour.'

They highlighted the differences between sending copies for review versus promotion. 'For reviews, authors can use e-copies of course, but at the moment the market is very competitive.

As there are new releases all the time, physical copies always work better in terms of visibility.'

Selecting the right book bloggers and bookstagrammers can feel like a black art. The Paper Charm team rely on their personal experience to make a selection. 'We're both influencers and we understand who likes what sort of book, and their review policies. Social media is not a single block – you have Twitter, YouTube, blogs, Instagram. Depending on the book, you may need to combine these platforms, or focus on one of them.

'There is no right answer to "how many?" – it depends on the book and the author. Every book is a different case… This depends on the author's previous work, their social media presence, the genre of the book and the book cover, of course.'

The Paper Charm gives hope to authors without much of a social media presence. 'Some authors have very little or no visibility on social media. We have authors who we help with this; together we plan the online persona and the kind of content they want to share, and provide guidance on social media.'

The Paper Charm cautioned against mass-mailing or reusing a list over and over again. 'We always hand-pick influencers/bloggers to send ARCs to. We had been book bloggers for nearly two years, and one of the things we immediately recognised is that in most cases the ARCs were not getting into the right hands. It's so time-consuming to pick and contact the right people so this is not anybody's fault. But I think making sure the ARCs go to the right people, the people who will read and review and share the love about them, is really crucial for the author.'

Lastly, I asked The Paper Charm about the biggest mistake they see authors making when it comes to Instagram and blog tours. They replied, 'Not thinking about the reach. These tours are not only for reviews, but they are also about "getting the word out". How many people will see your book by the end of the tour? If it's only a couple of hundred – is it really worth it? Also, it's important that the author interacts with the people who share their book. By that, I mean comments and likes, as a form of engagement with the people who are sharing content about their books.'

CHAPTER EIGHT

Making Social Media Work for You

Social media can be a great way to connect with fellow writers and find an audience of engaged readers. It can also be a black hole that delivers few returns. Like all other platforms, it requires an understanding of the algorithms that drive it, a genuine interest in using it regularly and a laser-like focus on the audience's interests rather than your own goals.

Authors can ignore social media, but do so at their peril. Nowadays it is almost a requirement that you at least have an online identity, one you ideally visit from time to time to show proof of life. If they harness it properly, authors can use social media to engage readers in real conversations, converting them from followers to fans to online friends.

Step 1: Get the basics right

When you create your social media accounts, start with getting the basics right. This means that you need to have your name clearly evidenced, include some kind of profile photo and header banner and, last but not least, a link to your website or other bookselling platform.

Don't be afraid to use both personal and professional accounts. Some platforms prioritise personal content, so you may find that your personal updates are reaching more people than your business page content, regardless of how many followers you have.

Next, add links to your social media accounts to your website, Amazon, Goodreads and any other place where you have a presence. This helps to verify that the new social accounts are indeed connected to you.

Once you've established your identity, start posting. It doesn't matter if you have zero followers; the point of posting is to show that you are committed to the platform and will be there to engage with anyone who turns up.

Step 2: Make genuine connections

There are two ways to build up a following, and you will need to do both. The first is to tell everyone you know that they can now connect with you on the new platform. This might be your newsletter subscribers, blog readers, email contact list or simply family and friends. Promote your social channels as an additional way to stay in touch, but not as a replacement for whatever they currently use.

You definitely do not want your email subscribers to stop opening your emails.

The second way to gain followers is to follow others. By others, I mean accounts that you genuinely like: fellow authors you enjoy reading, industry accounts, book reviewers and book bloggers. Not all of these accounts will follow you back, but some will. Either way, now that you will see their content in your feed, you have an opportunity to engage with them and start building a relationship. Even if they only see you liking and commenting and never respond, this may still make them more likely to recognise your name and open an email later on down the line. You must be authentic in your engagement – don't be afraid to respectfully disagree or comment on topics with your own perspective.

Some platforms, like Facebook and LinkedIn, offer online meeting spaces for groups. You should ask industry connections what groups they recommend as well as searching directly on the platforms themselves. Active groups provide great opportunities to interact with fellow authors, get tips and advice and see behind-the-scenes information on industry changes or news.

Step 3: Create a multi-pillar content plan

We all have that one friend who only posts photos of their dog. Sure, their dog is cute, but after the fifteenth photo in a week we'd like to see something else. Your author social media accounts are no different.

I recommend that users plan a strategy around a few content pillars. For example, you might have one pillar around books or reading in general, another around your story's themes, a third around you as the author and a final one centred on your readers. The content pillars act as guides for bringing a variety of content into your plan, and also ensure that you are trying to sell to your followers every time you post.

When it comes to selling, less is more. Literally. At least eighty per cent of the content you post should be for sheer entertainment or educational value, and some of this could be created by someone other than yourself. You can use links to articles or videos, memes or images. With the twenty per cent or less left, you can think about selling. You might promote someone else's book. You could showcase your promotional merchandise. You could let followers know about special offers, free downloads or newsletter giveaways. You can also promote your book. Be forewarned: most platforms limit the reach on any direct links to retail websites, meaning only a small fraction of your followers will see those posts. You may need to be clever in how you share information on where people can buy your book.

Step 4: Engage, engage, engage

This is the step that most business users get wrong. They forget that they are talking to real human beings on the other side and fail to engage. You should always be thinking about how you can elicit a response from your followers. You can ask questions, run polls or post memes that encourage people to respond.

As soon as you see responses come in, reply to them. This reconfirms to them that you are also a real human being. It also lets them know that they can use this channel to have a dialogue with you.

Over time, you will no doubt start to notice trends in who responds. Not everyone plays well in the social sandbox, and you should not hesitate to call out anyone who misbehaves, or even block them entirely. A zero-tolerance policy goes a long way towards fostering good communication with everyone else.

Take note of the individuals who regularly comment on, like or share your content. This is the group you can target for conversion into super fans. Ten super fans will deliver more value than 100 generic followers, so they are absolutely worth the investment. At some point, you may want to create your own group (on Facebook, for example) where people can engage in conversations with you and other followers. These super fans are the ones most likely to join in and drive the conversations. When the time comes to launch your book or announce a special offer, they will no doubt share the news with their friends and family because of the closer connection they have with you as an individual.

How Jen Mann uses social media to market her books

In Spring 2011, Jen Mann launched a blog that only her mother and friends read. With a degree in creative writing, Jen found that blogging provided her with an outlet to showcase her creative side. In December of that same year, she wrote a funny little post complaining about the Elf on the Shelf toy. That post was read by more than a million people in less than twenty-four hours. She had stumbled straight into success and her life changed almost overnight.

With a sizeable social media following, you would expect writer Jen to list Facebook as her most effective marketing channel.

'I've got over a million followers. I haven't sold a million books. You won't sell a copy to everyone who likes your social media accounts. The algorithms alone make it impossible to reach all your followers.'

Jen instead views platforms like Facebook, Twitter, Instagram, YouTube and Pinterest as audience engagement tools. 'I found my audience on Facebook and have built it up over the years. When my blog post went viral in 2011, I didn't even have a Facebook page. I rushed to create one and got to work posting up content and engaging with followers.'

Through steady hard work, she has built up a community of people who like what she has to say and trust her.

For Jen, the real value of social media is using it to find your super fans. Super fans are those people who will support you in everything you do. They will buy your books and recommend them to everyone they know. They are invested in your success.

'My personal Facebook account is my secret weapon. I keep my friends total just under the 5,000 friend limit. Everything I post on there is public, so anyone who isn't in my friends list can still follow me and see and engage with everything I put up. I've got 15,000 followers waiting for space to open up in my friends list.'

Jen now manages multiple Facebook pages and a myriad of Facebook groups, and has maxed out her personal Facebook friend capacity. In this way, she is able to game the algorithm and reach a much larger group than a page alone would allow.

'I set myself a target to get at least 1,000 super fans. They all know who I am and what I'm selling. I put in the effort to post up content and reply to threads. Most importantly, I am quick to cull the people who are not on board. A smaller group of super fans is much more valuable than a large group of people who don't know who you are or don't support you.'

She utilises the eighty/twenty rule when it comes to posting content on any of her social channels. Eighty per cent of the content is written by someone else – interesting articles, funny memes, book recommendations, etc. The remaining twenty per cent is for promoting her own work. 'I'm selling twenty per cent of the time, but not necessarily selling only my own work. I may promote a book that I think my audience will like. I am selling reading and building up trust. When I have a book coming out, I want them to remember that they usually like what I write and share.'

When it comes to social media, the bottom line is that you will only get out of it what you invest. Jen said, 'I spend half my day marketing myself, and half my day writing.'

CHAPTER NINE

Using Mailing Lists

Several years ago, agents and publishers looked for large social media followings to indicate sales potential. Nowadays, everyone is asking about your mailing list. It doesn't matter which publishing route you choose – your chances for success improve significantly if you can build up a mailing list of potential readers.

Newsletters have long been a common marketing strategy for businesses. Companies often attract sign-ups by promising special discounts or freebies, which allows them to build up a list of prospects they hope to convert to customers over time. They hire marketing teams to ensure that their newsletters go out regularly and include highly relevant and engaging content. They know that every single subscriber is a potential customer, and for those who have already converted and purchased something, newsletters help increase retention and repurchase rates. The strategy is no different when it comes to authors.

Thinking about running a newsletter for the rest of your life is a really good way to get overwhelmed and end up abandoning ship before you even get on board. To make this tactic manageable, I've broken it down into a series of steps and components. Work through each step before worrying too much about the next one.

Step 1: Is a newsletter right for me?

Yes, 100 per cent yes – a newsletter is right for every author who is planning to publish more than one book or short story. If you would like to enjoy return readers, a newsletter should be at the top of your marketing plan.

Step 2: Prep work

Before you even think about content, there are a few things you will need to prep in order to launch a newsletter. First up, you will need an email marketing provider and a newsletter registration form. These are the bare minimum. Most email marketing providers will include a registration form as part of their package, so don't stress if you don't have a website or don't know how to code. Once you've selected an email marketing provider, you will need some basic design support to make a newsletter header image and some images for your registration form. These will be your primary communication channels, so don't be afraid to spend a little money getting professional support if needed. Next, you should think about newsletter freebies. What can you use to entice readers to sign up for your newsletter and opt in to receiving regular emails from you? Free short stories or ebooks, special book discounts or fun swag like signed bookplates, bookmarks or T-shirts are all good ideas.

Step 3: Creating a template

Don't think about content, think about content blocks. Your newsletter template will be your guide every time you sit down to prepare a new edition. Instead of thinking about specific stories or blog posts you can share, move up to the level of theme or topic. For example, you might choose to have a short intro with timely information about you at the top, a link to a new blog post you've written underneath it, a list of books you're reading or that you recommend, a section promoting a specific book or short story of yours and a personalised sign-off at the bottom. This takes the guesswork out of newsletter content. You may also want to think about crowdsourcing content so that you don't have to write thousands of words for each issue. For example, you can share favourite articles you're reading, book reviews you've found, interviews with other authors (or cross-promotion), or even funny jokes or stories you've read and want to pass along.

As part of your research, you should subscribe to other author newsletters. Take a look at how different writers approach them, making a note of any ideas they inspire. You may find new content ideas or see opportunities to organise newsletter swaps where you cross-promote each other's books.

Step 4: The automated funnel

Kristen Mae and Meghan O'Flynn, who spoke with me about how they use newsletters to sell books, were excited to talk to me about their automated subscriber funnel. This is not the same as the newsletter itself – your automated funnel is a series of two or more emails that you set up to automatically go out to anyone who signs up for your mailing list. These emails will run in the background, ensuring you never forget to welcome new subscribers. These are not artificial; they need to be genuine and specific, showing your readers that you care about them and value their willingness to give you their email address. The first email should, wherever possible, include a free item they cannot get anywhere else. This is the incentive to sign up in the first place. This email should always thank subscribers for signing up, should set expectations for what else they will receive (no spam, special offers and content just for you, behind the scenes access, etc.) and should provide the freebie. If you have an additional freebie you can offer, such as another short story or ebook, save this for a second automated email.

The next email in the series could be an introduction to you as the author. Tell them about yourself, what you like and dislike, your approach to writing, what you like to read – anything that lets them see past a name on a book cover. This is your chance to be one human speaking to another: use it! After that, you might want to send an email letting people know where they can engage with you online. Meghan and Kristen both promote places like Goodreads, Amazon and BookBub with the promise that their readers will never miss out on a new release. You may want to include social media links as well, particularly if you have an active private group on a platform they can join.

Step 5: Scheduling your funnel

I asked Meghan how she spaces out her automated emails. She said, 'Everyone has a different wait time depending on whether I included something for them to read. There's no point in me sending out another email if they haven't had time to finish what I sent in the previous one.' I like Meghan's advice because it gets us away from feeling pressured to adhere to specific sending days or overly engineered plans. The funnel should feel natural, as though you are personally hitting send on every email. There is no deadline for getting them out and no necessity to pick a special day of the week or month.

Step 6: Regular updates and other newsletters

Thousands, if not hundreds of thousands, of dollars and pounds of research and analysis has gone into understanding which day and time of the week deliver the highest email open and read rates. What I've found in all my years of experience is that a really well-planned and well-executed newsletter, with engaging and relevant content, is effective any time you send it out. You are not a faceless company sending out a mass email, you are one human emailing a group of friends. When you've got something interesting to say, you can send out a newsletter or update. You've already created a template and have content blocks to fill. When you've hit a critical mass of information to pass along, you are ready to send out a newsletter.

How many is too many? If you have a number of exciting or important events happening in a week, combine these into one email. If you've got a couple within a month, you can split these up into multiple emails. Put yourself in the recipient's shoes – if you received these emails, would you be annoyed and want to unsubscribe? If so, hold off until you've got better or more content.

How many is too few? Personally, I believe that three or four per year is the minimum number of newsletters you need to send out to help people remember that they signed up to your mailing list in the first place. If you go too long without sending one (six months or more in most cases), people will forget that they chose to subscribe – or even that they know who you are and like you – and this will drive up your unsubscribe rates. It's like committing to a new friendship: if you meet once for coffee and don't see each other again for a year, you probably won't make an effort the next time around.

Step 7: Promote, promote, promote

Who should you tell about your newsletter? Everyone. Put it on your website. Link to and promote it on your social channels. Put it in your author bio and in the back matter of every book you publish. If you have an online author profile, list it there. Your newsletter mailing list is your most prized possession – you should always be thinking about how you can grow it.

How Meghan O'Flynn and Kristen Mae use newsletters to sell books

Meghan O'Flynn and Kristen Mae met when they were new to the blogging scene. They honed their writing chops through blog posts and freelance articles before getting up the courage to try novel-length writing. Having a large audience of engaged fans certainly didn't hurt when the time came to release their first books. However, despite the fact that they have thousands of social media followers, Facebook isn't their biggest marketing tool. Meghan's *Ash Park* series and Kristen's *Conch Garden* series have both earned the Amazon bestseller badge multiple times, thanks in part to their newsletter funnel strategy. Their writing partnership extends into marketing as well, with the two of them sharing best practices or even diving in to help each other. I got in touch to find out what they know about newsletter marketing.

Kristen started off by describing the difference between their newsletters and their funnel. 'The funnel is what everyone gets when they join our mailing lists.'

'When you sign up for my newsletter, you will automatically be sent a series of twelve emails,' explained Meghan. 'The first email includes a free short story that my readers can't get anywhere else. The second email pushes my first book, which is free. This way they've got two freebies straight away before I hit them with anything else.'

Meghan's emails are spaced out to give the recipients time to take advantage of whatever reading opportunity she is offering. Reading is definitely the keyword. Every newsletter is centred around the idea that the recipient wants to read or wants to discuss what they're reading. Even her email about her webshop talks books, as all of her promotional items include fan-favourite lines and book covers.

tlet, Brownie brought these products
ers' homes, demonstrating how they
erting her prospects into buyers on the
he was hired by Earl Tupper, the inventor
as his vice president of marketing. Books
exact same way if you can identify where you
ether small groups of readers at a low cost.
oting down key characteristics of your typical
w old are they? What are their hobbies and in-
here do they go for either fun and entertainment
ion and improvement? For example, if your book
popular with business people, you might note that
tend breakfast meetings, break for lunch and some-
gather for networking drinks. All of these natural
ering points provide you with a starting place for plan-
g your next step.

ep 2: Determine a budget and breakeven point

Grassroots marketing, like all the other marketing tactics,
does require some investment. You can seek to minimise
costs by choosing free venues and convincing someone else
to pay for any food or drink requirements. However, you
will still need to cover at least the cost of your time and your
transport. Before you go any further with your planning,
work out a budget.

Kriste

new

form

social

profiles.

them inclu

hook readers

a connection b

reminding them o

When I asked th

debut authors, they bo

Kristen quickly follov

a writing partner. Megha

revisions of each other's work

This helped us get our books in

an editor to review, and it meant

traditional retail o

directly to consu

worked and con

spot. From this,

of Tupperware

can be sold th

can gather to

Start by

readers. H

terests? W

or educa

is most

they at

times

gath

nin

S

Once you have a rough budget in mind, divide it by the amount you earn per book sold. This is your breakeven point. Ideally, you want your breakeven point to be reasonably within reach of a small to medium-sized group of attendees. You can use your breakeven point to establish a minimum number of guaranteed pre-sales required for an event to take place.

Step 3: Plan your typical event

The goal of your grassroots events is to convert your customers into your brand and book ambassadors. You want them to leave with a copy of your book, a great impression of you as an individual and a desire to help you achieve your goals.

In order to do this, you must be authentic. You cannot expect to turn up at an event and portray yourself as someone you are not. Put together an event plan which capitalises on your strengths and allows the audience to experience you at your best.

Your book will sit at the core of your event plan. What excerpt might you read to give the audience a sense of your writing? What story can you tell about the book – perhaps sharing insights into your writing process, inspiration or things you learned about yourself along the way? Make sure you plan to tell the audience what success looks like for you and what it would mean to achieve it. You want them to know what your dream is and what they can do to help you reach it.

The remainder of the event plan should focus on engagement. What questions can you ask to get the audience talking to you and with one another? You should also think about movement, making sure you don't leave the audience sitting for an extended period.

Last but not least, plan to personalise autographs and hand out promotional materials. Each attendee should leave with something in hand to show that they have met and connected with you.

Step 4: Ask for hosts

Had Brownie Wise only hosted parties on her own patio, the Tupperware brand certainly wouldn't be a household name. Your success with grassroots marketing will come from connecting with eager hosts who are capable of bringing a group of people together.

Once you've exhausted your circle of friends and family, you should ask around for hosts. This is where your newsletter subscribers and social media followers come in handy. Send out a note to let your fans know you are ready to travel, providing detailed information on where you can go and what you need from them.

Step 5: Publicise the event, both before and after

Successful events breed more successful events. Use every avenue available to promote your events in the days leading up to them. Once the day arrives, take photos, note down stories and encourage your attendees to do the same. After the event is over, write a wrap-up post to share on your website, in your newsletter and on your social channels. Namecheck people you met, share anecdotes and include photos. Make sure everyone who follows you is aware of how fun, educational, entertaining or informative the experience of meeting you is.

How Jen Mann uses grassroots marketing to sell her books

Jen Mann jumped from small-time blogger to internet superstar overnight when over a million people read her satirical blog post about the Elf on the Shelf. Over the years, Jen has turned her blog 'People I Want to Punch in the Throat' into a publishing empire.

Jen has built up her social media following to over a million, thanks to her willingness to tell it like it is and her very savvy marketing skills. On top of short stories, she's published six books of her own and seven anthologies featuring a collective of fellow bloggers, utilising both traditional publishing and self-publishing channels and achieving commercial success and accolades galore. The secret to Jen's success: she fosters deeply personal connections with her readers.

Like many traditionally published authors, Jen's first foray into book tours was the traditional brick-and-mortar bookstore signing. She travelled around the US, sitting in bookstores and hoping someone would come by to see her. She quickly realised that this approach wasn't appealing to her target audience.

Jen explained, 'I really didn't want to do another traditional tour, and I made a joke that I'd rather meet a group of friends in a bar or at someone's home than sit in another empty room. My inbox quickly filled up with invitations.' She had a hit guerrilla marketing idea on her hands, and now needed to figure out how to make it work financially.

'My husband and I did some calculations and identified that if I could use low-cost airlines, free venues and inexpensive accommodation, twenty-five pre-sold books was the magic number I needed to make a trip break even.' Since then, she's travelled back and forth across the US, meeting readers in homes, community centres, bars, churches, restaurants and any other free venue her host selects. She's eschewed the traditional big cities, taking her roadshow to small towns where her loyal fans are thrilled to get a chance to host her and introduce her to all of their friends and family.

'It helps that I have so many different titles I can take with me – people end up buying multiple titles and buying books to give to friends. I take around five titles to each event so that I can upsell to people on the spot.'

Travelling from town to town can be gruelling and Jen learned the hard way that rest time is important. 'When I started, I would fly in, do an event in the evening and fly to the next town the following morning. I made myself sick. Now I make sure to build in rest time. I plan to stay in a town for two to three days. I have a part-time assistant who helps me find additional speaking opportunities in the same area. It might be a local women's group or a library. She has a list of topics I can cover and aims to book two events per day. Sometimes I get paid for the speaking events, on top of them being opportunities to sell more books in the same trip.'

Jen's one piece of advice to debut authors is pretty simple. 'Enjoy it! It is a big deal. Only once do you get to be a debut author and fulfil that dream you had of publishing a book. Live in that moment. Revel in it.'

CHAPTER ELEVEN

Jumping on a Viral Trend

Executing a marketing and promotional strategy centred on a viral trend is fairly easy. It's trying to put an advance plan together to create one that is hard.

Nowadays it seems as though half of our news feeds are filled with 'viral' stories and videos, with millions of views and thousands of conversations happening almost instantaneously. When that clock starts ticking, you have to act fast if you hope to capitalise on a viral theme or else think hard about how to turn a viral moment into a movement.

Step 1: Read and watch everything (related to your topic)

If you hope to sell copies of your book off the back of a viral idea or story, you need to know about it as soon as it starts to take off. To do this, you have two options. The first is to read and watch everything remotely related to your book topic. Easy, right? If you find this too much of a challenge, you can use resources like Google Alerts and your book's fans.

Google Alerts allow you to identify a set of keywords to track on the internet. Whenever the Google search engine identifies new content containing your keywords, you get sent an alert so that you can check it out. Google Alerts are a useful tool for anyone in the public eye – as an author you should at minimum set one up using your name and book title(s) as the keywords. Based on my personal experience with them, the alerts won't catch everything and may take up to a day or two to arrive. If you need immediate alerts, there are more expensive press or social media monitoring tools.

If you have an open dialogue channel with your fans, such as a Facebook or LinkedIn group, often they will let you know if they've seen something that reminds them of you or your book.

Step 2: Look for commentary opportunities

Every day, thousands of journalists are writing articles that require third-party commentary. With deadlines hanging over their heads, they turn to Google searches, Twitter requests and websites like Help a Reporter Out (HARO). You can use these same tools to identify opportunities to provide a journalist with commentary and promote your book at the same time.

Once again, keyword alerts and hashtag tracking are your best aids in finding these opportunities. I recommend adding email alerts on top of your own monitoring, as time is typically of the essence when these calls go out. You must be able to respond quickly and concisely, explaining who you are, your relevant expertise or experience and your availability to provide a comment. Don't forget to add in your contact details.

Your comment may or may not be used, so don't expect every opportunity to result in press coverage. This is a numbers game and your hope is that you could be at the crest of a viral wave.

Step 3: Move fast

I cannot stress enough how important it is to move quickly if you see an opportunity to capitalise on a viral trend. Very few viral trends grow into a movement. Most fizzle out within a few days. With no way to know how quickly a trend will be replaced by the next big thing, if you see an opportunity you do not have the luxury of dithering over whether or not to use it.

To drive home this point, I will show you how I leapt onto a viral trend and used it to sell copies of a book. In late May 2015, everyone was talking about the upcoming release of a new memoir (*Primates of Park Avenue* by Wednesday

Martin), which promised a behind-the-scenes look at the elite housewives of the Upper East Side of New York City. Three days before the book was released, the *New York Post* ran an article by an Upper East Side elite housewife justifying her life. It immediately went viral. Three thousand miles away, I read the article and quickly saw an opportunity to enter the discussion. Whilst I was far from an elite housewife, I saw how I could use my own experience to move the discussion along. I quickly penned a personal essay and submitted it to the *Huffington Post*. The editor published the post within a day and it went on to become one of the most read articles on the *Huffington Post* that year. The entire timeline from the first article to my own was five days. My response was the last article on the topic to go viral.

Step 4: Link to everything and don't forget to name-drop

The viral trend is the open door, but it is up to you to make the most of it. The only way to do this is to mention your book title and, where possible, link to your website. If you are providing a quote, try to include phrases like 'In my book, XYZ' or 'This inspired my book, XYZ'. If you weave it into the main body, it is less likely to get left on the cutting-room floor.

If, like me, you have the chance to write a response article of your own, include links to your website within the body of the text and make sure you have your book title listed clearly in your author bio. Make it as easy as possible for anyone interested to find your book for sale. In my case, I immediately saw a resulting spike in sales.

Step 5: Making the most of a movement

In some rare instances a viral trend will catch on and spark a movement. Clean eating and KonMari are excellent examples – in both cases the initial articles caught everyone's attention. What made them different and lasting is that they generated a multitude of conversations that continually advance the trends and keep them from fading away.

Movements provide you with the luxury of time, although not an infinite amount. If you have already written a book that is relevant, you may want to consider hiring a public relations expert to help you maximise the commentary opportunities. If you are writing a book but it is not yet published, you will want to fast-track your process and make sure you highlight your connection with the movement when searching for an agent or publisher, or when writing marketing materials for self-published work.

How Olga Mecking used a viral trend to land a book deal and market her book

Olga Mecking's writing career started when she launched a blog. She found she enjoyed the writing, putting more and more time into crafting blog posts and hoping she'd eventually go viral and find a way to make money from her hobby.

She discovered that going viral takes a lot more than talent. It is like being struck by lightning – you have to be in the right place at the right time, but the odds are still a million to one. Over the years, Olga grew her skillset, pitching story ideas to big websites, studying their content and figuring out how to write articles that resonate with mass audiences. She learned more than just writing: she discovered how to spot quirky ideas that would appeal to audiences and editors alike. When she saw an article on the Dutch wellness trend *niksen*, she knew she was onto something.

'I first wrote about *niksen* for *Woolly* magazine, after seeing a call for pitches in a Facebook group. The article did really well on their site. A few months later, I saw another call, this time for the *New York Times* Smarter Living section. I emailed the editor my idea. He asked some follow-up questions and then declined. I kept writing and pitching, and a few months later he got back in touch. That never happens! He wanted the article on *niksen*. It took months to get through the editing process and wait for publication. The editor only promised to run it online, thinking it wasn't a good fit for print. Then the article came out.'

Olga's *New York Times* article on *niksen* went viral, with nearly 100,000 social media shares in the first week. *Niksen* was suddenly everywhere, in the US and abroad, and Olga was

ce where you set your book, you
both localities.

ther an outreach group

your hometown, you need to be ready to
nnection you have to help promote your
you know, who do they know and how can
connections for marketing purposes?
ilar when thinking about where you set your
ve you visited the place or do you have friends
y in the area? Did any local individuals or groups
ou with your research? Are there any other writers in
ar genres who call that locale home? If so, these are all
nnections you could use in building up your outreach plan.

Your outreach group should be broken into three
audiences: people you can send a press release to (such as
editors at local news outlets), people you could approach
with a more formal letter or call (such as booksellers and
potential event hosts), and finally people who you call friends
or acquaintances.

Step 3: Building an outreach plan for your audiences

Outreach to your first audience is fairly straightforward.
You should write a short press release which promotes your
connection to local readers. Your press release should include

now the expert. 'I began thinking I could turn the article into
a book deal, but when I looked into the process of finding an
agent and then a publisher, I got discouraged by the amount
of work and how long it would take with no guarantees.'

What Olga didn't know was that the agents and publishers would come to her. Within a month of the article
coming out, she had multiple requests for proposals, leading
to offers and a deal.

Traditional publishing timelines often last two or more
years for a debut author. This isn't the case when you are
trying to capitalise on a viral trend. 'When you are writing a
book on a viral topic, the timelines are really aggressive. The
original article came out in May, and the book launch is less
than a year later. I wrote my first draft in six weeks and will
finish the entire book in less than six months.

'I'm always thinking about how I can keep *niksen* in the
news, and keep up momentum around the book itself. When
I write a chapter, I'm thinking about what else I could do
with that information or where I might pitch a freelance
article on the same theme.

'*Niksen* had all the building blocks to go viral. It plays to
a number of popular trends, like minimalism, wellness and
international ideals like the Danish *hygge*. The Netherlands
consistently ranks as one of the happiest cultures on Earth –
I knew people would want to know how they do it.'

Olga's one piece of advice to fellow writers is to look at the world as she does.

'The best stories aren't obvious. They can be quirky or hyperlocal or what your friends and family are all talking about on social media. Each time something makes you stop and say, "Wait, what?" and want to learn more, you may have a story. Keep your eyes open everywhere.

'Remember, stories don't always present themselves in one round. Sometimes they come in pieces, and it might take you years to find all the parts you need to tell it. Keep looking and storing away ideas until you can see how they fit together.'

Marketers frequen[...] that make national cam[...] this happens, they use 'hyp[...]

Hyperlocal means focusing [...] efforts in a select number of town[...] maximising reach and engagement w[...] budget. You can also call it community [...] people often start with the communities where t[...] and work, or where they have a large number of frie[...] and supporters.

Here is a guide to how you can use hyperlocal marketing to promote your book on a minimal budget.

Step 1: Select your region

You will want to look at two options for selecting your locality: your own area and your book's setting. Unless you

information about you, your book, the local connection and where the book can be bought. You may also want to source a quote from a local influencer, such as a bookstore owner, book reviewer or notable resident. Don't forget to send along a headshot and/or a picture of your book cover. Once you've prepared your release, send it to the relevant email address and monitor the local news outlets to see if it gets picked up.

Outreach to your second audience requires striking a balance between professional and personal. This audience might include local bookstores and libraries, book clubs, networking associations, writers' groups and any other organisation that might consider stocking, selling or promoting your book. Before you contact anyone, check to see if they have listed a preferred contact method on their website or social channels. Draft a set of talking points and a personalised letter you can send out, repurposing some of the content you put into your press release. Don't forget to let them know if you are or will be in the area and can sign books or host an event.

The third audience is the easiest. Now is the time to call in any favours and beg for a helping hand from everyone you know. This will be easier if you provide them with all of the tools they need to market on your behalf. For example, start a Facebook conversation with local friends to ask for their help, and include a link to a post on your own page that they can quickly share. You should ask them to include a note at the top letting their friends and families know about their connection with you. Ask them to request the book in bookstores and libraries they frequent and to recommend it to any clubs in which they participate. You can also send them an email they can forward to their address book.

Step 4: Return the favour

This is the most important step in any hyperlocal campaign, as it signifies that you are a thoughtful and respectful member of the local community. Think about ways you can give back to the people, businesses and groups who have shown you support. Can you promote their businesses on your social media accounts? Can you share information about their clubs or activities with your followers? Can you promote one of their upcoming events?

Mentoring is another excellent way to repay people who have helped you gain success. Now that your book is out in the world, can you share the insights you've gained along the way with people around you? You might attend an event or put together a short seminar. The more involved you are in helping the entire community succeed, the more willing people will be to return the favour.

How Emma Timpany used a hyperlocal campaign to market her book

Building up a local network happened very organically for Emma Timpany. As a newcomer to the Cornish coast, she joined a number of local writing groups as a way of making connections and getting feedback on her own work. She published her first short story in 2010, won two prizes for short story writing in 2011 and from there was on her way towards a respected literary writing career.

As her confidence and experience grew, she signed up for Telltales, a well-established group of readers and listeners based in Falmouth in the UK. Telltales allowed her the chance to read her work to an audience, seeing first-hand how they reacted and mastering presentation skills. In addition to finding an audience, she also gained friendships with other local writers and connected to the large following and social media network Telltales had created over many years.

'Live reading events like Telltales create a safe atmosphere for new writers, as the focus is on listening to other people's work. You can start off as a listener and see how other writers perform before going up yourself,' explained Emma. Staying in the network for years, as a listener, reader and eventually as one of the organisers, Emma gained a community of readers long before she published her first book. 'People support you and become long-term friends or acquaintances. Everyone wants everyone else to do well.'

In 2018, Emma had two books published. The first was *Cornish Short Stories: A Collection of Contemporary Cornish Writing*, an anthology of short stories which she both edited and contributed to. The second was her novella *Travelling in the Dark*. Emma activated her local networks to promote both.

'The short story anthology came out first. My co-editor and I together organised over twenty events throughout Cornwall, with small groups of contributors coming along to read and participate.

'My co-editor had worked at a local bookshop, the gorgeous Falmouth Bookseller, for many years, a great connection which meant that they were happy to host the launch event. When my novella came out, I contacted them again and they kindly agreed to have me back. Local connections like this opened doors to networks that often operate on a personal level. I was able to book events at shops because I knew the people who worked there or had connected with them at writing events.'

Emma leveraged locally run book festivals and book prizes as well. 'Festivals are great for raising awareness of you as an author. They are often competitive to get into, so being accepted acts as a validation of your work. You can reach a whole new audience through their marketing.

Additionally, local booksellers will often partner up to provide books for sale at festivals and prize readings. This gives you a chance to get your book onto their shelves.'

In her role as a mentor, Emma often looks for opportunities for debut authors to make a name for themselves. When she spotted a new literary prize for writing from her region, she forwarded it on to a friend with a recommendation that they enter. They turned around and made the same suggestion back to her. The exchange ended up being fortuitous as Emma's novella went on to win the top honours in the UK's 2019 Hall and Woodhouse DLF Writing Prize, launched the previous year by the Dorchester Literary Festival to recognise writing from the West Country. It is no surprise, therefore, that Emma is quick to point to hyperlocal marketing as a key to her own success.

Emma had a few pieces of advice to pass along to debut and emerging writers:

'First, remember to treat every book as unique, and take time to think about what is special about that particular work. You can often reuse elements of your marketing plans, but focusing on the books individually will help you create the strongest plan for each book.'

Her second point concerns the writing community at large. 'Help and encourage other writers. The community runs in a circle, and you will get back what you put into it, even if it comes back in an indirect way.'

Her final piece of advice is important. 'Take time to celebrate getting your book published. It is a special day when books are born into the world, and it deserves recognition.'

CHAPTER THIRTEEN

Book Prizes

Book and writing prizes may not seem like a logical place to start your marketing; however, there are some very good reasons why you might want to move competitions up to the top of your marketing plan.

For debut authors, competitions can provide you with invaluable opportunities to gain feedback, connect with other writers and identify potential mentors and critique partners. By moving prizes and writing competitions to the top of your list, you'll have additional tools in your promotional arsenal as well as a team of cheering supporters.

Step 1: Doing your research

Everyone has heard of the major literary prizes, but what about the hundreds of smaller competitions that happen around the globe? Before you start paying entry fees, do your research into what opportunities exist for your work.

A logical starting point is your genre. Many genre-specific associations run annual prizes and monthly or weekly challenges for both members and debuting authors alike. Competitions can be an excellent way of gaining access to insider information from associations that only allow published authors to join.

You don't need to have a fully edited novel ready before you enter competitions. There are prizes for short stories, flash fiction and best first chapters, and even specialised awards like best romantic scenes. Entering your work into these types of competitions can gain you critiques and feedback that you can make use of before you submit to an agent or hit publish.

Step 2: Selecting competitions

With so many writing competitions available for your consideration, I suggest that you compile a list of options first. Putting them into a spreadsheet can make it easy to sort them by deadline or category further down the road. Make sure you check the entry requirements, as some prizes are not open to self-published authors and require publisher submission. Some prizes are more focused on self-published or traditionally published works, and others may allow both.

As many prizes require an entry fee, you will want to have some sort of criteria for determining where to invest your money. Start by looking at the competition website, checking for information on the judges and past winners. It isn't necessary that you see a recognisable name. Instead, look into the types of works that are being recognised. If they are high-calibre writing in a similar style to your own, the competition may be a good fit for you.

You should also look into what the prize entails and if there is any reward for writers who don't place. For example, is there a long- or shortlist which recognises a larger group of entrants? Do the judges provide feedback or scores on each entry? Are there online or offline networking opportunities? Note the answers to all of these questions in your tracking spreadsheet.

Step 3: Submitting your work

Submitting your work to a competition requires more than simply clicking a button on a website. Before you prepare your submission, make sure you closely review the submission guidelines. Competitions may require documents in a specific format, or may offer the option of sending additional materials such as query letters or synopses for review.

If you fail to follow the submission guidelines, your work could be rejected or you could automatically lose points.

While submitting before the competition deadline is an obvious requirement, don't immediately discard a great opportunity simply because the deadline is close or has just passed. If you are within a day or two of a deadline for a competition you think is a good fit, you can contact the organiser to see if there is any flexibility. This won't work everywhere and should not be a go-to method, but you can try it as a one-off for smaller competitions.

Step 4: Making the most of competition networking opportunities

Once you have entered a competition, keep careful note of any networking opportunities. If there is an online community, join it and actively participate. If there are offline, local or regional events, attend the ones in your area.

Networking opportunities are not the time to shy away from self-promotion. Be prepared to talk about yourself and your work, be honest about your capabilities and don't hesitate to ask for what you need. For example, if you are looking for a mentor or a writing partner, put a callout within the group. You may find others who are in a similar position but were hesitant to admit it.

Follow your fellow entrants on social media, read their work and celebrate their successes.

Step 5: Promoting your prize

Should you be fortunate enough to win a prize, get ready to promote it using every channel available.

The best place to start your promotion is with the competition organisers. Ask them what promotion they do and what tools they can provide. For example, they may send out press releases or provide press release templates for your use. They may also have custom graphics made or social media sharing templates and hashtags you can leverage.

Next on your list are updates. You should update your website and social channels with news of your win. You may want to swap out your social media cover images or add logos to your website sidebars. You should also update your book's pitch sheet. If possible and appropriate, you may want to update your book cover to showcase the prize.

Now that your own promotional materials are up to date, you should begin telling the rest of the world about your good news. At the top of your list are either agents (if you do not yet have a publisher) or bookstores (if your book is available). Use the prize to open doors that might otherwise be closed to you. For example, if it is a local prize, bookstores in the local area may have dedicated displays for highlighting winners. If it is a national prize, you can use the win as a good reason to get in touch with booksellers who don't stock your book. It is much the same with agents – seeing that your writing has been validated already could move you up the consideration list.

How Sophie van Llewyn leveraged her award wins to market her book

By the time Sophie van Llewyn published her first book, she was no stranger to prizes and competitions. They have played a key role in her own personal development as a writer, and ultimately have had a major impact on the commercial success of her work.

Sophie was always passionate about writing long-form content, but her early attempts at writing novels left her uninspired. To gain more experience and find a community of fellow writers to support her, Sophie started entering short story and flash fiction competitions.

Sophie explained, 'I was living in Germany and didn't have anyone with whom I could share my writing. I started following short story prizes on Twitter, expanded into flash fiction and eventually joined the Bath Flash Fiction community. It was a great way to meet people. They have weekly writing prompts and online workshops, giving me plenty of opportunities to meet other writers and to improve my own skills.'

Sophie discovered a talent for writing flash fiction, eventually assembling fifty-one flash pieces into her first book, *Bottled Goods*. While each 'flash' can be read as a standalone, together they tell an overarching story.

Sophie's success with smaller writing prizes convinced her publisher to submit her book for two of the major UK book prizes, the Women's Prize for Fiction and the People's Book Prize. She was longlisted for both of these prizes, an incredible achievement for a debut author, and particularly important for her as a writer of literary fiction. *Bottled Goods* was also longlisted for the Republic of Consciousness Prize in 2019, a prize specifically designed for indie publishers.

'Being longlisted made my book visible. Major booksellers had dedicated shelves at the front of the store where they displayed the longlisted titles for the Women's Prize. This gave me access to new booksellers and made me stand out. It also helped me attract foreign publishers. We've sold publishing rights to Harper Perennial in the US and Canada, and to Keller Editore in Italy, as well as to Audible for the creation of an audiobook.'

Her publisher supported her marketing efforts with updated images for her social channels and website. 'I decided to invest in a new website as I knew more people would be searching for information about me. It was definitely worth it as my site traffic increased by thirty per cent following the announcement.'

Sophie also worked with her publisher's PR agent, drawing up a list of themes she could write about that related to her book. The PR agent pitched the ideas to publications, and Sophie was able to write an article for *Mslexia*, one of the UK's major women's writing magazines, which was both informative and promotional.

Competition deadlines still fuel Sophie's writing and she highly recommends new writers consider entering short story and flash fiction contests. She explained, 'You can get your writing out there more quickly, get feedback and join a community.'

When asked for her one piece of advice, Sophie didn't hesitate. 'Don't give up. There will be days when you think your writing is terrible. It will be hard and there can be a lot of rejection. But you can do it if you put in the hard work. Every writer I know doubts themselves, even if they've made a bestseller list. Moan, pick yourself back up and get back to work.'

CHAPTER FOURTEEN

Hiring an Expert

As a marketing director with commercial targets and limited budgets, I am constantly looking for the best way to achieve my objectives. In some cases, the best course of action is to call in specialist external support. The same holds true for book marketing.

Hiring an external marketing or PR expert can be a great way to take advantage of promotional tactics that are outside of your skillset or comfort zone. They can fill gaps in your execution plan or help you take a step back and re-evaluate what you've done to date. If you're struggling from the outset or your sales have stalled, it may be time to call in an expert.

Step 1: Identifying the expertise you need

In my experience, the hardest part has always been coming up with a shortlist of agencies to query. The best way to start is to take time to think through exactly what support you need. Do you need help with online marketing, such as Facebook, Twitter or Amazon ads? Do you need creative materials or a website refresh? Could a publicist or PR agency help put you in front of new audiences?

Make a list of every tactic you've tried to date and note whether they worked well (i.e. achieved your target or paid back any investment). Anything that hasn't delivered or any gaps are good places to start your search for external support.

Once you have an idea of your specific needs, reach out to your network of fellow writers for recommendations. Make note of their feedback, both good and bad. You can then supplement their lists with online research. Sometimes it is more useful to know who not to ask than it is to have a lukewarm recommendation.

Step 2: Writing a brief

Before contacting any agencies or experts, you should prepare a short project brief. This will ensure that the agencies know what you want and can prepare comparable proposals for you to consider.

Your brief should include an overview of your book, including genre, publication date and publisher, and any sales data you feel comfortable sharing. You should provide a summary of what you've done to date or plan to do to market your book. You should make clear what types of specific support you need.

Next, share any deadlines or key milestones you expect them to meet, specify deliverables (particularly if you need design services) and detail your budget.

Step 3: Requesting quotes and proposals

You should always endeavour to get at least two quotes or proposals before you select an agency or consultant. This means you'll need to send out three or more requests for price quotes or proposals. If you have a specific request for a deliverable or standardised service, you can ask for a quote. If you aren't sure what support you need, you can ask for a proposal instead.

It is reasonable and appropriate to ask anyone you query to include their credentials and examples of relevant work from their portfolio. It is not reasonable to ask people to provide you with a bespoke pitch pack with creative examples for free.

Make sure you send out your requests with enough turnaround time for them to complete the proposal. Good agencies and consultants will have other projects on their plate, and may need days or weeks to work up your proposal. Depending on your deadlines, you can either assign everyone the same deadline or ask them what would be reasonable.

Step 4: Evaluating quotes and proposals

When hiring an agency, I always find it helpful to give everyone the same deadline and to set time aside to read all submissions in one go. This ensures that I give them an equal amount of my attention and can keep them all fresh in my head. If you have more than two or three to consider, you might want to create a quick scorecard to make comparison easier.

As you look through your options, you should consider the following criteria:

- Have they met your requirements?
- Can they work within your budget?
- Can they meet your deadlines?
- Does their approach allow you time for feedback before the project is done?
- Do they have experience or specific expertise you value?
- Were they able to demonstrate previous similar work?

Step 5: Hiring an agency or consultant

Once you've selected your external support, formalise your agreement with a contract and a written project description. Depending on the type of support you need, the contract could range from a paragraph up to a dozen or more pages. The agency or consultant should provide a contract for you to sign – make sure you read it carefully before agreeing so there are no surprises down the line.

The project description should detail the type of work being done, deliverables, deadlines and fees.

Step 6: Communication

Your evaluation process should ensure that whoever you hire is capable of doing the work. Getting it done, however, depends on your communication skills. Don't expect to sign a contract and send them on their way. Set aside time for a briefing call and be prepared to answer questions, provide information and share any necessary creative assets. The sooner you can give the agency or consultant all the information they need, the more likely you are to get good results quickly.

How Alexa Bigwarfe helps writers market their books

When you find yourself in over your head or short on time, you can turn to people like Alexa Bigwarfe. Alexa owns the company WritePublishSell, where she helps authors with everything from writing to publishing to marketing and promotion. Alexa explained, 'There are a lot of areas of expertise required in publishing, from graphic design to editing, understanding Amazon metadata, and on into marketing and promotion. It takes a lot of time to develop a real understanding of the industry, so if you don't have time or aren't interested, bringing in a guide can be a big help.'

Alexa was quick to point out that hiring an expert doesn't mean that you're handing control of your book over to someone else. 'An expert can help you shortcut the process and still keep control.'

The biggest mistake Alexa sees authors make when it comes to marketing is not understanding their audience. Authors need to focus on building up their own mailing list, learning what their audience likes and then using it to match their book and their marketing approach to their audience's preferences. She said, 'You would not believe how many people come over who have had a big "uh oh" and now need help.'

Alexa has plenty of advice for authors who want to lean on companies like hers to support their marketing efforts and increase their chances of success. She recommends that authors prepare well for the initial call, to save time and get the most value from it. Ideally, come ready to talk about what you have done already to market your book. Have social media, website and Amazon links to hand or send them over in advance. Last, but definitely not least, share any insights you have from your own mailing list and newsletter experience.

Once Alexa has heard from the author, she then does her own research. 'I do a deep audit. I check out the author's social media accounts, looking at their content and their engagement rates. I will subscribe to their newsletter and see what I get back. Only then will I start to put together a plan, capitalising on what they do best and offering support with the rest.'

When it comes to finding an expert like Alexa, she suggests people start with referrals. 'Ask your network where they've gone for support. You will hear horror stories – push past them. Keep looking until you find a company that people you know are happy to recommend.'

And if you don't have a network, Alexa advised, 'You can also ask an agency for referrals if they are either too expensive or not a good fit for what you need. We have a network of freelancers and other companies we use regularly and know people can rely upon.'

For Alexa, the bottom line is this: 'We have our best success when we stay in our own lanes. Do what you do best, and outsource the rest. Don't waste valuable time doing things badly.'

I asked Alexa for her one piece of advice to debut and emerging authors. She said, 'Start marketing as early as you possibly can. It's hard work to grow an audience and it is only getting harder. Above writing, editing and everything else, start building an audience.'

CHAPTER FIFTEEN

Crowdfunding

Most marketing tactics cost money. When you view your book as a business, you may need additional investment to get it off the ground. If you don't have deep pockets, you may need to think creatively about how to find investors in your book marketing activities. Some people also use crowdfunding to produce their book.

In 2012, well-known blogger Seth Godin decided to turn to crowdfunding to generate funds for the production and promotion of his book. He launched a campaign on Kickstarter, aiming to achieve $40,000 in pre-sales from his engaged audience of followers. By the end of his thirty-day campaign, he'd crowdfunded a remarkable $287,342 in pre-sales of a book he hadn't yet written. Not only did he surpass his target, he demonstrated how authors can use crowdfunding to drum up interest and activate an audience of investor-readers.

According to the Kickstarter website, the 'Publishing'

category has seen over 48,000 projects raise over \$173M. But only slightly more than thirty per cent have reached their target. As an all-or-nothing platform, that means only thirty per cent of people who have tried to crowdfund money for their book have managed to get any. It is possible, but it is far from a guaranteed way to get funding for your marketing activities.

Step 1: Approach a crowdfunding audience as you would any serious investor

Regardless of whether you are hitting up a wealthy aunt, applying to a bank, pitching to an investment house or crowdfunding, you need to take the pitch process seriously. You are, in essence, asking someone to help fund you in getting your business off the ground. The fact that your business is a book makes no difference.

Start by doing your research up front. Some platforms require you to reach your target before you see any of the money. Others allow you to cash out even if you miss your goal. You will also want to look into the usability and credibility of the site. Make sure you know what you are getting into before you make a selection.

Step 2: Get an audience

Crowdfunding requires a crowd. No platform in the world will deliver this to you. If you want to have a chance at success, you need to have an audience in place who you can engage and encourage to help you achieve success. This is why so many successful bloggers look to crowdfunding when they decide to write a book. They have a large audience of engaged readers who have been enjoying their content for free for an extended period. These bloggers generate excitement around the idea of a big chunk of fresh writing for their audience, who already love to read their work.

Step 3: Prepare your audience for the launch

Once you've selected a platform, set a goal and got an audience in place, now is the time to educate your followers on what to do. Crowdfunding a book isn't like buying a copy online. The book won't show up at their house the next day. Equally, it isn't like raising money for a cause or charity. You aren't asking for donations. Everyone who invests gets something in return, but only if you achieve your target.

Well before you launch your campaign, you need to begin prepping your audience on what action you want them to take. You obviously want them to pledge, but you may also want them to spread the word by promoting your campaign on their social channels and by word of mouth. Either subtly or overtly, you must educate them on what to say and do. You want to ensure they know that the campaign is time-sensitive and that they aren't making a donation but an investment.

Step 4: Prepare your campaign page

The quickest way to fail at crowdfunding is to skip setting up a professional campaign page. This is not the time to cut corners. Look through successful campaigns in the category to get an idea of what you need and what the platform algorithm is supporting. You should expect to need photos, preferably a professionally edited video, stellar descriptions and coveted rewards.

Step 5: Build up a thirty-day marketing plan

If you are shy about promoting your book, crowdfunding is not for you. From the moment the campaign goes live until the second before it closes, you must be a marketing machine. Due to the time-sensitive nature of this tactic, you will want to prepare as much as possible in advance. Stockpile a variety of photos and graphics, write new blog posts or newsletter stories, prepare newsletter templates and plan ahead for milestone updates. If you already have a communications platform in place, you may have a good idea of what gets your followers engaging – whether it be a personal essay, a funny meme or a live video. Nonetheless, you need to be prepared to shift your tactics if you find your audience's preferences change when it comes to spending money.

Step 6: Launch with instructions

In the lead-up to launch, move education to the forefront of your communications plan. Tell your audience what you are doing, how much you need to raise and exactly what you need them to do. Above all else, make it clear they need to act fast. Getting proof of early interest is required if you want a chance at success. This proof might be hitting a certain number of backers, achieving a target number of pre-sales or even generating a large amount of support and shares on social media. The first twenty-four to forty-eight hours of your campaign are critical for gathering evidence that people believe in your mission and your goal, so that you can share this on your campaign page.

For the remainder of the campaign, be prepared to be annoying. You may find yourself posting ten times a day on social media, sending out multiple newsletters and personal emails, phoning up everyone you know or even paying to increase the reach of your social media posts. Use every channel available and use them often, varying content until you identify which types work best.

How Lisa Ferland uses crowdfunding to market books

Lisa Ferland has successfully funded two books on Kickstarter – an anthology of stories called *Knocked Up*

Again and a children's book called *When the Clock ⎯s on Halloween: A Cute Rhyming Tale* – generating $15,000 of investment to help bring her projects to ⎯blication. She now works with authors to guide and support them through the crowdfunding process, helping them raise a total of over $150,000 in investment.

Lisa knows first-hand how important it is to take the process seriously. 'Like any marketing effort, crowdfunding isn't something that you should ever try on a whim. What's worked really well is when an author has taken the time to build an audience, to get them super excited about their crowdfunding campaign's launch day and to incentivise people to share the campaign with their friends.'

Lisa explained that the key to the campaign is coming up with interesting rewards and incentives. 'I've seen creators give away additional ebooks (other titles) and create other digital rewards as incentives for sharing the campaign with friends. I've also seen them offer book bundles, Skype interviews and short story freebies. It is important to give them something more than they could get if they ordered your book on Amazon.'

When I asked Lisa how you can apply crowdfunding tactics to book marketing, she was quick to reply: 'Crowdfunding IS marketing – it's just a sprint instead of a marathon. All of the material generated for a crowdfunding campaign can po…

, podca…

the campaig…

r to promote the…

ve, there isn't a ton of…

quickly that changing mar…

s can make a huge difference…

et. In short, don't be afraid to ch…

t working.'

The experience of quickly analysing what is…

king comes in handy when your book is avail…

e. Lisa told me, 'Another key takeaway from crowdf…

g is that you learn really quickly what marketing messages

orked and didn't work during your campaign. You can see

ery visually which rewards people wanted (and which ones

were ignored) and that can help you make decisions about

which types of formats or extras to offer in the future. For

example, if you offered a really cool T-shirt that embodies

the message of your book or character and nobody selects

it during the crowdfunding campaign, you know not to

produce a ton of T-shirts.'

Lisa's willingness to take risks comes through loud and

clear in her one piece of advice for debut and emerging

authors. 'Don't be afraid to look silly. It takes a long time to

find what works for you, so you have to try a lot of different

s at
good at
o be open-r
rying new thin

After your publication date has passed, if your marketing efforts have started to flag, take your lead from the retail world. Black Friday, Small Business Saturday, the White Sale – all of these are great examples of how the retail world leverages holidays and other seasonal events to increase sales

When it comes to promoting your book, you may not have a large back catalogue of material or a warehouse full of items you can discount. This doesn't mean you can't use a seasonal theme to market your work.

Step 1: Think outside the book

Unless your book is holiday themed, you'll likely have to look outside its cover to create a seasonal connection. Put your book behind you and place yourself into the minds of your readers. As the season or holiday approaches, what will they be thinking about that you can leverage in your marketing?

...ns to contain ever more

...ople to purchase presents.

...ays, Mother's Day and Father's

...ays and more are all opportunities

...o promote your book as an ideal gift.

...rom the long summer holidays to shorter-

...breaks, vacation seasons offer readers the

...rfect excuse to indulge in a new book.

...Weather: when temperatures drop or the rains pick

up, people are looking for an excuse to stay inside.

You can use this as a chance to suggest your book.

Step 2: Preparing your promotional materials

The only downside to seasonal promotions is that s...

stores do them. Inevitably, you're going to be ...

crowded market. That doesn't mean you shoul...

instead think about what you can do to st...

You will want to prepare custom ...

in advance. Think about images ...

special newsletter editions and ...

Make sure your prospective ...

of what you have to offer ...

You can help you...

promotional item...

and inexpens...

be repurposed at a later date for ongoing marketing efforts. Articles, podcast interviews and graphics that went live during the campaign can always be reshared throughout the year to promote the book. Since crowdfunding is time-sensitive, there isn't a ton of time to experiment. You discover very quickly that changing marketing messages, graphics or outlets can make a huge difference in the number of backers you get. In short, don't be afraid to change things if they aren't working.'

The experience of quickly analysing what is and is not working comes in handy when your book is available for sale. Lisa told me, 'Another key takeaway from crowdfunding is that you learn really quickly what marketing messages worked and didn't work during your campaign. You can see very visually which rewards people wanted (and which ones were ignored) and that can help you make decisions about which types of formats or extras to offer in the future. For example, if you offered a really cool T-shirt that embodies the message of your book or character and nobody selects it during the crowdfunding campaign, you know not to produce a ton of T-shirts.'

Lisa's willingness to take risks comes through loud and clear in her one piece of advice for debut and emerging authors. 'Don't be afraid to look silly. It takes a long time to find what works for you, so you have to try a lot of different techniques before you discover what works best. You will never know if you have a great radio voice if you never do a podcast interview. You'll feel ridiculous at first, but it's only with repeated practice that we get good at anything.

'I'd encourage all authors to be open-minded, conduct a ton of research, and keep trying new things.'

CHAPTER SIXTEEN

Keeping up the Momentum

After your publication date has passed, if your marketing efforts have started to flag, take your lead from the retail world. Black Friday, Small Business Saturday, the White Sale – all of these are great examples of how the retail world leverages holidays and other seasonal events to increase sales.

When it comes to promoting your book, you may not have a large back catalogue of material or a warehouse full of items you can discount. This doesn't mean you can't use a seasonal theme to market your work.

Step 1: Think outside the book

Unless your book is holiday themed, you'll likely have to look outside its cover to create a seasonal connection. Put your book behind you and place yourself into the minds of your readers. As the season or holiday approaches, what will they be thinking about that you can leverage in your marketing?

- Gift-giving: the calendar seems to contain ever more holidays which require people to purchase presents. Christmas and birthdays, Mother's Day and Father's Day, recognition days and more are all opportunities you can use to promote your book as an ideal gift.
- Vacation: from the long summer holidays to shorter-term breaks, vacation seasons offer readers the perfect excuse to indulge in a new book.
- Weather: when temperatures drop or the rains pick up, people are looking for an excuse to stay inside. You can use this as a chance to suggest your book.

Step 2: Preparing your promotional materials

The only downside to seasonal promotions is that so many stores do them. Inevitably, you're going to be entering a crowded market. That doesn't mean you should skip out, but instead think about what you can do to stand out.

You will want to prepare custom promotional material in advance. Think about images for your social channels, special newsletter editions and pinned posts on your website. Make sure your prospective reader gets plenty of reminders of what you have to offer.

You can help your book stand out by including special promotional items with each sale. These can be as simple and inexpensive as autographing books or sending out signed bookplates. You could write a special short story that is only available to seasonal purchasers. If you have control over pricing, you might introduce a short-term discount or package up a bundle.

Step 3: Relaunch your marketing

Releasing a seasonal promotion can be just as important as your initial book launch. Revisit your original marketing plan and see what ideas you can reuse. Can your street teams help you spread the word? Can you write more articles for external publications? Could you use this as a reason to reach out to booksellers?

Seasonal and holiday marketing campaigns require effort, and should be supported with an updated plan of activities and timeline of milestones. Pick and choose which seasonal promotion opportunities best align with your book, genre or audience rather than trying to force your book to fit into all of them.

In the business world, when product sales begin to flag there is one obvious solution: introduce a new product. It is the same in the publishing world. Every multi-book author I interviewed cited their backlist as one of their most effective marketing strategies.

Rather than provide a step-by-step guide for this tactic, I have provided options for ways you can build up a backlist more quickly than simply writing another standalone title.